If You Love Me

Me

Chris Haley

Dedication

To all those who continue to search

Contents

Sitting at the Bar With Another

Before we were introduced,
I knew I'd love you.
You didn't know I was looking,
So, left unseen, I kept peeking.
I thought there is my dream,
My wish upon a star.
I shuddered at the possibility
That suddenly, so near,
I might have found
What always seemed so far.

Greetings

I said, "Hello."
With the touch of your hand
My pulse raced a hundred yard dash.

It crossed the finish line when you said,
"Nice to meet you."
And I collapsed,
A winner at last.

Everyday

If every day
Like Deja vu
I met you,
And everyday
there was just us two,
Then everyday
I would relish my life,
By sharing every day
With you.

Show Me Now

Teach me how to love you.
Show me what I should do.
Instruct me on the dos and don'ts,
So one day you'll fall in love with me,
Like I already have with you.

It's Your Choice

Choose whatever you want.
Hit up the best restaurant and eat yourself silly.
Binge your favorite series until your eyes get blurry.
Visit the swankiest resort and stay in bed till three.
Choose whatever, your options are free.
The only thing I ask is,
Let one of the options you choose
Be me.

You Leave Me Breathless

Falling in love
Is almost as magical
And intoxicating,
As falling apart
Is brutal
And suffocating.
Both experiences
Leave you

Breathless.

Sweet Breath

Kiss me with all you've got,
My air is in limited supply.
If my last breath is spent loving you,
There's no sweeter way
To say goodbye .
Let them say my last day
Was caused by lips
That took my breath away.

Kiss Me Again

When you kissed me that first time,
My knees went weak.

When you kissed me the second time,
I sensed we wouldn't be getting a lick of sleep.

When you kissed me the third time,
I felt I was at home.

When you kissed me the fourth time,
I realized I'd never be alone.

You

The most romantic word
I say
When you're with me,
Is the same word
I say
When you're away,

Your name.

Don't Worry, My Love

If you love me,
That's all you need to do.
You don't have to buy gifts.
You don't have to promise bliss.
You don't have to greet me
When I come home
With an embrace and a kiss.
If you love me,
That's it.
If you love me,
Nothing else exists.
If you love me
I'll love you.

Who am I kidding?

I already do.

Why

Why? You ask me.

You're the best feeling I ever felt.
You're the best hand I've ever been dealt.
You're my rainbow in every sky.
You're the reason romantic movies
Make me cry.
You're the reason I gave love
One more try.
You're the hand I pray I'm holding
The day I die.

You are my why.

Songbook

Now you're here.
I can hardly believe it.
We are we;
I no longer say,
"No. It's only me."
With our cats, our doormat,
Our big screen tv,
We have a couch, a kitchen,
And a bedroom.
We have a porch
Where we can wave at our neighbors, daily.
Singing the same sad song so long,
I forgot there were other melodies.
Finally, I have a new songbook
To join my old cookbook.
I guess patience was
The best recipe.

Forget Me Not

You being in my life
Has caused the only bout of
Forgetfulness,
I am glad to have had.
You make me so happy

That I don't remember ever being sad.

Because I Know You Care

When I come home
And you are there,
I smile inside
Because I know you care.
We laugh.
We eat.
We stay up late.
I am proud of everything we share,
Because when I come home
And you are there,
I feel love;
I know you care.

Perfect Dreams

If I had let go
Of my perfect dreams,
If I had set aside
My technicolor movie scenes,
If I had seen you for what you were
And not how novelists wrote you should be,
We'd be chilling together
With Netflix,
Actually watching tv.
If I had let myself love you
And not the idea
Of a perfect dream.

For Another You

If I could find the words
To catch another soul like you,
If words were all I had to use,
I'd devour the English language
And become multilingual and fluid
In the rest of the world's too.
Then I'd write and I'd shout
Until my red heart turned blue,
If words were all I could use
To catch another soul like you.

A Love Song For You

I wish I could write
A love song for you.
It might be made up of lies,
But the intent would be true.
To manifest my dreams of us,
I'd write you still love me
As I still love you.
It might be wishful thinking,
But what else have I to do?
Goodbye, my love.
I wish I could have written
A love song for you.

One Try

I'd like to see your eyes
One more time,
Like my heart saw them that day
When breath opened my lips
And I said "Hello."
I think we'd forget we've said goodbye.

I've long since forgotten why.

Won't you let me try?

Wordsmith

Some of the most beautiful words
I've ever written
No longer have meaning,
Because they were all written
About you.
Now you're gone
And my words left with you.

Flags Have Two Sides

Crazy
When you realize
The same flirty flag
Which drew you in,
Was the warning sign
You should have heeded
When you decide this
Shit has to end.

You Left Me Breathless

Words can't strangle the pain I felt
The moment I became aware.
You told me you awoke one morning
After someone else had stripped you bare.
And you enjoyed it.
I trembled like the temperature was zero.
My stomach hit the floor.
The love I had for you
Smothered me.
I couldn't think.
I couldn't breathe.
I hated you
And wanted you more.

Listen to Me!

Many friends said
You were wrong for me.
Therapists earned thousands of dollars
Advising me to leave.
My heart kept saying
You would change.
It persuaded my mind to believe your loving claims.
Days, weeks, and months passed;
I kept hearing the same.
But you didn't change.
My brain continued to drain.

Who you listen to
Can be open, closed, and easy,
Or expensive, exhaustive, and needy,
When you recklessly rehash memories
With cash dipped in disdain.

French Kiss

You doubted me
From the moment you ogled my fleshy lips.
You thought you'd taste them
And leave after a sloppy French kiss.
But I bit yours first
And licked them.
Then you couldn't get off my stick.
Until our flavor dried up
Like an old tube of Chapstick.
Then we spit each other out
With not even one last
 sip.

Table Setting

When I sat down at that table
And you sat across from me,
I wondered if we'd share wine one night,
I wondered if we'd share a sunrise one day.

I wondered if we'd share a future
Beyond this particular afternoon,
Which might span many anniversaries.

Our sunrises only lasted months,
But our friendship has lasted years.
I never imagined that could be,
When I sat down at that table
And you sat across from me.

For The Last Time

If I could hold you
One more time,
Like I held you the first time,
And the embrace could remind me
Of our good times,
I would hold you
Like you were still mine.
I would hold you
Until we felt fine.
All this I swear I'd do,
If I could hold you
One more time.

For Better or Worse

I'll want you around,
When we're old and gray.
I'll want you around,
When we're bent and lame.
I'll want you around,
When we can't remember our names.

Our bodies and brains may soften,
But as long as our hearts pound,
There's no doubt in my mind,
I'll want you around.